There Is A Solution

. . .

The Beauty of Recovery

by

Amanda Sloboda

Bloomington, IN  Milton Keynes, UK

AuthorHouse™
1663 Liberty Drive, Suite 200
Bloomington, IN 47403
www.authorhouse.com
Phone: 1-800-839-8640

AuthorHouse™ UK Ltd.
500 Avebury Boulevard
Central Milton Keynes, MK9 2BE
www.authorhouse.co.uk
Phone: 08001974150

First published by AuthorHouse 2/27/2007

ISBN: 978-1-4259-9624-6 (sc)

Printed in the United States of America
Bloomington, Indiana

This book is printed on acid-free paper.

Acknowledgments

. . .

This book has been written for those fortunate looking for experience, strength and hope. If you are reading this book, you are truly a miracle. Anyone with one day of sobriety has a chance. I have taken the time to write this in hope that one person may find the freedom and find a life they could never imagine. A special thank you, to all of my friends for making this possible. A special thanks to my love, Brian for allowing me to have the courage to get out of my comfort zone and make this happen.

My Experience

...

I will begin this with how this journey has occurred for me. I will admit, that I never thought it possible for a sick person like myself to find peace and change. I am only twenty-five years old and I typically do not find many people my age in the rooms of recovery. I started down the path of disaster at a very young age. Serious decision making errors occurred, as I never made positive decisions while my addiction had me under its wrath. I had a horrible attitude, I never had any stability and I just went from one friend's house to the next, as I never had a home. I never paid rent until I had some recovery under my belt. I never had a car or a job, I just totaled one car after another, and my side of the story never included what part of it was my part. I never apologized to any of my friends or family when I was wrong, which today I see I was wrong most of the time. My attitude and my perspectives were always wrong, as I have always worn tinted glasses as I was in denial for a long time. My friends and family never trusted me while I was in my addiction, as they knew my character defects included lying, cheating, and stealing. So, most of the time I was living in cars that belonged to the people that took care of me. Even during the winter, I lived under these conditions.

My addiction ruined all areas of my life. Spiritually, emotionally, financially, I was completely bankrupt. This "friend" of mine had turned on me. At first, I wasn't always loaded. However, this disease is progressive. At first, I was just drinking to unwind or at parties and it wasn't in large amounts. However, it progressed very quickly and before I knew it I didn't do anything without my alcohol and or my drug of choice.

In order to walk through the door to finding recovery, I had to loose everything. I lost homes, family members, friends, money, jobs, and any material thing I got my hand on. I never thought I had a problem with alcohol or drugs. I was the last one to know. All of the people that touched me tried to tell me and offer me help. Though, I was not ready until I was ready. When it came to my disease, I just couldn't grasp the concept of recovery, my addictions, or how simply I had the opportunity to change.

One of the big things that continued my denial was that I had this concept of what an addict was. My preconceived notions of what an addict was a person that stood on the street with a sign that read homeless need money. Everyone knows what I am describing. Someone that has not had a bath in weeks, has no material items, not even what it takes to live. People that have no clothing, home or simply the things that it take to get along in today's world. The type of person that you know doesn't need money for food or clothing. It's obvious that they are just looking for their next high.

So, in my addiction, I wasn't out begging for money. Though, I sure was looking for the next parties, high, drink or any mind-altering chemical. I thought that because I had people taking care of my every need that I didn't have a problem. One of the big reasons I came in and out of the rooms almost like there was a revolving door in front of the rooms, was simply because I kept thinking I was trying this deal. When in reality, all I was doing was picking up that first chip that seemed to give me the go ahead to just continue down my road of destruction and misery.

An outward sign of an inward commitment, when I heard this I thought a commitment was in the context of a relationship and I sure knew nothing about that. As, I had no idea what the definition of commitment was. I was not making a commitment to the program or to getting myself well. I just continually picked up those white chips, and used them as a commitment to continuing using my drug of choice.

When I went to meetings, I would go loaded, or get loaded after the meeting. I didn't listen to anything anyone suggested as I thought I was being told how to live my life. Don't you know, that nobody was going to tell this outlaw how to live. If I had just came in and listened for sixty minutes. I hated those stupid sayings on the wall when today those sayings save my life. As, prior to genuinely giving myself to the program I lived in a self made prison. Today I am living, not an animal. For the first time, I have found genuine happiness.

In my addiction, I lived a pretty rough life. I never had any money. To be honest, looking back at my life when I was at the height of my drinking and drugging, I merely existed. I was not eating, showering, sleeping or doing anything that productive members of society do.

My family was always worried about me. People truly loved me and I was horrible to those that genuinely tried to help me out. They tried to get me to stay at home and become productive. However, I had to go through what I had to go through. As, when my friends and family were trying to help me and coerce me to go to rehab or go to meetings, I simply was not ready yet.

I was stuck in my addiction for twelve years. I did have days when I didn't use. I would quit for a few days. I would quit when I didn't have the money, the weather was too bad for me to go out, when I couldn't manipulate people to get me my stuff or when I was sick. However, I was stuck in the cycle of addiction. At the beginning it was fun, until I had to use alcohol and drugs to function.

I was never able to take care of myself while in my addiction. I didn't get the concept of paying bills and being a productive member of society until I had approximately a year of sobriety. While I was sick in my addiction, people clothed me, watched over me, fed me, and gave me whatever I needed. I was over twenty-one, an adult, and I never held and/or kept a decent job. I could not keep hold of anything. I would get jobs and they only lasted a short time because they got in the way of my addiction and I always had an excuse why I couldn't keep a job.

This was a cycle that I was stuck in for most of my addiction. I would get material things and loose them within weeks. I never had any living or coping skills and I just never understood why I could never get my life straight. Also, I was always in trouble and in and out of institutions.

I always blamed the parties or people, places and things. I always had excuses for anything that happened that was negative. I never saw my part in anything that happened. The cable or the electric would be cut off and it was always the cable company's fault. It was always every body else's fault. I always thought in these situations that these companies just hated me and just decided to cut off my services for no reason. When it was really that my checks bounced or I didn't bother to go up there and pay these companies for their services.

I would do anything to get high or drunk and stay that way. Once I hit my high, I would do things that I normally would never do. I would do anything, and pay any price for my drugs, they were that important to me. I would go to any length to get high and stay high. I never considered how many miles I had to drive or whether I had to go to dangerous places to get high and stay high. I would trust people with my money when I didn't know them to get alcohol or drugs. I lost money this way on more occasions than I would like to admit.

I had no concept of being a productive member of society. I simply thought that productive members of society were only "normal" people and "squares". I considered productive members of society people that never had any fun.

It took what it took for me to genuinely go to meetings and stop drinking and everything and work on me. I literally lost everything to the disease of addiction. I lost homes, jobs, family, friends, lovers, when I was using and/or drinking I couldn't keep anything.

Quite literally when I arrived at the rooms of recovery I had a little tote bag and hardly nothing in it. Though, that is what it took for me to become willing. The difference between when I was made to go into recovery and when I wanted to go were like night and day. When I went in for all the wrong reasons it was just a show.

When I actually dragged myself in the door genuinely, it was totally different. As, I was willing to do anything to be sober as I was working on dying. However, after all the bottoms I had and the bottom fell out, I found out there was an alternative. I have been around the program for a good long while. I came to meetings loaded. Or I would go to meetings and get loaded after the meeting. I had some serious patterns. I would get into trouble and I would have my mom or other close friends clean up my messes, as I never paid any consequences.

Due to not paying any consequences, I personally think I stayed out longer than necessary. I was in denial. I didn't see that I was not just hurting myself. As I thought my addiction was hurting only me. It took me a long while to understand that when I pick up not only do I loose but the people around me loose also. I was so far in denial that I didn't realize that I had more liabilities in my life than assets. As at this point, I had only a handful of assets.

At first, I had my own opinion of the program. I thought it was a cult. I didn't and couldn't find an hour a day to learn about my problems. As, I thought if I went to these meetings that people would judge me. I hated coming in over and over picking up white chips. I thought the program was a form of brain washing. I was not open minded, willing or honest.

The reason I was not open minded willing or honest was that I had spent so much time behaving insanely; I was just doing the same things over and over again and expecting different results. I thought that this higher power was going to be something extreme. I was expecting skywriting or a burning bush. As, don't you know, I was unique.

What do you mean I needed to get involved and hang out with a bunch of sick alcoholics and addicts? I didn't get the idea that these people in the rooms for the most part could tell my story. These people had not only walked in my shoes, but they knew there was an alternative, a solution to the insane way I was living.

In the beginning of my recovery, I had totally missed the boat. I resisted and I tried to hold onto old ideas. I wanted to continue being a rebel. I could not see that some of the people that had been around for a while could teach me how to live sober and that I didn't have to be loaded or live the way I had been living for so long that I was comfortable with. I didn't believe that I could change. I did not see that I could change my old ways and enjoy life and trade my negativity for positivity.

The only way that I was able to make major progress in the process of stopping self-judgment and getting rid of the toxic shame was to become conscious of the bigger perspective. When I began believing that a higher power, a universal force, existed that was genuinely all-powerful and unconditionally loving, then life started to become a lot easier and more enjoyable. Then, I could begin to see that the misfortune and luck are really miracles and that these are merely opportunities for growth

The Change

...

So, how did a close-minded rebel like myself find out that life could be this good? I truly believe that it takes what it takes. I have proof from those "friends" out there that are trying to find a way to continue their drug of choice with conjunction with working the program that once you quit doing the old behavior and you get a mind full of information about recovery and you go back out it just keeps getting worse.

Those friends of mine that swore they wouldn't do hardcore drugs like IV drugs found out that if they quit their drug of choice and it got bad enough they would do any drug out there. Not to mention I have seen people have double digits that went back out and did some research and died to this disease.

Sure you can say I just smoke a little pot. However, provided that you are an addict, and you have a disease that keeps escalating, this is a progressive illness. This disease escalates at a very fast pace. The thing that people need to understand is that when you come into recovery and stop "the old game". Once you start again, you don't start over, you start over where you were miserable before, and it just gets worse and worse at a very fast pace.

In my experience, I kept going back for more, so who knows what would happen if I went back out. Honestly after how hard it was for me to get the time I have today, I don't believe I have another recovery. I don't think I have any more chances, as I believe I already found the last house on the block to find sobriety. Not to mention, if I chose to pick up today, there is no question about what I would loose and what the consequences would be. I have lost everything enough.

In my experience, I upset the people who were enabling me and cleaning up my messes. Such as my mom, my family, my friends, etc, they got tired of trying to help me when I truly didn't want any help. I had not had enough at that time. People would send me to meetings; find me a sponsor, the typical thing. I would do talk the talk, make people hear what they wanted to hear and continue to use. The reason I don't consider this continuing to relapse is that I was just continuing my using. I had made no attempt to stop and stay stopped.

I kept walking in and out the door of recovery for a decent amount of time. As, I personally was not interested in sobriety. I thought by having any amount of time in the program meant I would have no fun, and I would become a square.

Boy was I totally off the mark. Today I have a great life. I get to enjoy a lot of things. I just came back from an excellent vacation. I went to Orlando and go-to-go to not just a theme park as usual, I got to go to Disney right before Christmas, got to stay in a beautiful timeshare, hot tubs, and the works. I have managed to go to school, life has not quite been handed to me yet and it is a daily struggle. I will be dealing with my addictions for the rest of my life.

However, my dreams are coming true thanks to recovery. I still have some wreckage of my past. There are some things that I have done that I will never be able to make up to people. I did some terrible things to family and friends in my past. The only things I can do for that is engage in living amends and stay sober and do the right things.

When I came into recovery I had about a hundred issues and I had a ton of resentments. However, once I worked the steps and talked to others these things no longer have the power over me. I truly believe that the more I work my program, the better things get. In the dark of my disaster, there were some really crazy things that happened.

Relapse Not Required

. . .

Another thing I want to make sure I address is that relapse is not a requirement. I hear it a lot in the room about people that come and go all of the time. Relapse is not necessary. When I relapsed with nine months of sobriety, it was horrible. I lost all of my material things that I had had in the past. I lost things that my mom had given me, and she has passed away. Of course none of that stuff meant anything to me when I was messed up.

The thing that a lot of people think about recovery is that once they have some time and they make the decision to relapse, they have this idea that it will be different this time. For me recovery is a decision. As, certain things happen in my experience of relapse. I had a lot of pain, emotional and physical pain. The man that I loved had gotten involved with another woman. She wasn't a very positive woman. It wasn't a healthy relationship. For a long time, I was living in the past, the future; I refused to live in today. I was jealous that this man that I loved so much was in my mind cheating on me. I was feeling a lot of grief, and I was dealing with depression.

The big things that I did to cause myself my relapse was that I stopped using the tools. I moved, a geographical move, so in my mind I had a reason to relapse, because I couldn't remain teachable. I couldn't ask for help. So, as a result that I couldn't tell anyone in this new place that I needed to know where the meetings were in this new place, I chose to relapse.

My pride got in the way. The reason I say I chose to relapse was that I saw the relapse happening before it happened. It was much like dropping glass in the kitchen. Instead of catching, it watching it in slow motion, break.

I saw the warning signs but this three-fold disease stopped me from being teachable. I could have picked up the phone, and called someone. The thing that I normally don't admit to is that when I moved to Texas, I didn't move to Texas for the right reasons. I moved to Texas, because I wanted to get my stuff back. I moved to Texas, with a "understanding" that if I moved to Texas, and got myself back together that I might have a chance to find out what a healthy relationship with this man was.

So, I understand about my relapse showing me that I have to be sober for me. Not to show my old using buddies that I don't party anymore, not to show my parents that I'm sober, I have to do the deal of recovery for myself and to know me.

The Realization

. . .

I can't do recovery for stupid reasons or add all these stipulations on recovery. As when I add conditions to my recovery, things don't go well. Such as when I say I will stay sober today but if certain things happen I don't see myself staying sober. As, this means I didn't work the first step thoroughly. As, my sponsor today is hard core, and the first thing she asked me when I talked to her about recovery was if I had worked the twelve steps thoroughly and this is when I realized that I hadn't worked the steps thoroughly and that I was going to need to make a decision. Was I going to get into action and stop quitting on me?

Self-Affirmations

. . .

Love yourself, regardless of all the other relationships in your life. As you spend the majority of your time in the day with yourself. If you cannot or will not create that functional, stable relationship then you will have trouble living the quality of life you desire. Do become your number one fan, and enjoy spending time with yourself. Take time out to be good to yourself.

Take time out of your busy life to look around your environment. Spend a few minutes looking around you and take in all that nature offers. The other day, it finally occurred to me, that I spend much of my time with tunnel vision getting from point A to point B. I hardly ever look side to side or up and down. There's a lot to miss sometimes during the bad days or the sad moments to recall why we are happy to have the lives we do. Generally, the other side of the street is more alluring and we fail to comprehend that along the way we've cultivated exactly who we want to be and exactly the lives we want, even if we don't realize it, and we allow other influences to deter us from seeing the beauty. When we feel bitter or angry the last thing we want to do is make a gratitude list when you don't use the whole spectrum and beauty around yourself.

The cool thing in recovery is we can start our day over at any time. We have the ability to turn our days and wills over at any time during the day. Waking up on the wrong side of the bed often used to influence our entire days because we let it. Pause, take a deep breath and modify your thoughts, turn your anxiety, anger or sadness over to your higher power and begin again.

These are many ways I have learned of helping myself be a better friend to myself. There is no secret that we are our worst critics and the more we slow down and find out how to love ourselves with the care and compassion that we show other people the better off our quality becomes. There is nothing selfish or self-serving in taking care of our minds and bodies, of understanding the times when we need to be alone or be with others. The more we work on ourselves the more the people, places and things in our lives will fall into place around us with ease.

Where It All Began

...

So, what was my experience? My story was that I didn't have a bottom. It wasn't just one thing that happened. I had a lot of anger and resentments. As a big part of my drinking and drugging was that I was running form myself. My drinking began at a very early age. People in my family drank. To prove that one was that there is a wine overseas with my last name on it. Which, I jokingly say, well, that explains why everyone in my family drinks. When I know that that is just a joke. People in my family drink because they like to drink and stay drunk.

My family likes to party, so I was introduced to alcohol at an early age. My parents are alcoholics, my grandparents on my father's side are alcoholics and my mom's father has problems with alcohol. My aunts, my uncles, everyone that I know in my family enjoy drinking. So, alcohol was everywhere, in my family. Every holiday, any celebration involved drinking. I think it was before middle school that I had my first drink. From the time I was in grade school, there was always a keg of beer at my house.

My parents didn't watch the children; they really weren't adults in my opinion. Due to the alcoholism, I don't blame these people today, I just accept that they were sick people and our family is dysfunctional. I don't deal with these people today, and I don't want people to read this and say that I have anger issues or resentments. As, when I was a child I was a victim, as I didn't ask for the things that happened to me to happen. I trusted that these adults had some judgment and were decent people. I also want people that have walked in my shoes to see how I got through some of this stuff. My sister was less than ten years old changing diapers. I haven't met anyone today that didn't have a dysfunctional family. That doesn't make coming from a dysfunctional family right by any means. It's just where my story began.

So, I was dealing with my alcoholism for many years. I just never saw it as a gateway drug. The reason I say that my alcoholism was a gateway drug for me is that I seem to have a cycle of getting into my drug of choice, a pattern. My disease lies to me and I think I can just drink casually and before I know it I am caught up in my old way of life.

So, I started out just drinking and thinking it was a normal thing to do. Then, I was in high school and my close friends loved coming over to my house, as there weren't any rules at my house. It was pretty much a free for all when it came to alcohol. At this point I was thinking I was just drinking on the weekends. As it really was any time I was celebrating, and the weekends. By this time my alcohol was really my best friend. The only time I didn't drink at this time was when I was at school, at work or anywhere else that didn't permit my drinking. As, I was drinking so I didn't feel any emotions. When I was drinking I didn't hear anything that was going on at home. At this point I was raising myself. At the age of fourteen, fifteen, I already had me a little job, and I was going to school. I had my heart set on college.

As, I was sick and tired of being sick and tired. I was tired of the emotional turmoil that was at home. My mom had already sent me to three different therapists, so she could go to therapists and it looked good. My mom was really sick at this time. She was in her late forties, living in the past of her twenties. At this point I was really trying to not be like my family. There was so much crap that we didn't talk about at home. So, due to not acknowledging things at home, I was just reliving history and I was really pissed off about it.

The Insanity

...

By this time, I had lived through a lot. Family members that were supposed to protect me from the "monsters" in my family didn't protect me. I was a young girl living the life of an adult at a very young age. I had literally had my youth stolen from me.

By the time I was ready to go to college, I had lived as an adult for about six years, though I had lived through things that a child should never see. When my father chose to go back to school when he got out of the military, my life as I had known it went up in smoke.

I was a young girl and I was very confused at the time. My innocence was stolen from me and at the time I honestly was in denial and I thought my understanding of what had happened was inaccurate. As these monsters that my parents allowed into my life took my life away and they were very good at putting blame on a young child.

It took me years to recover from those things that should have never happened to me. Emotional abuse, physical abuse, and all avenues of abuse had hit me over a long period of time. My innocence was stolen from me over a long period of time. I never thought I would recover from the horrible things that happened to me. The worst part of it was that I was made to think it was my fault. As my parents told me when I went to them that when things like this happen to people, it was my fault, because I let things happen to me. When, I just wasn't strong enough to stop this horrible cycle of abuse that I was attacked by.

I am here to say that by getting years of outside help, and educating myself about abuse, today I understand that I was not at fault. I did not ask for what happened to me. I was merely a child at the time, and I trusted people that took advantage of my trust. I hated men for a long time. I didn't trust people for a long time. I chose to be alone for a while. This abuse that happened to me killed me for a couple of years. It stole my joy.

The reason that I have included this is that I have spoken to many people in recovery that hold themselves responsible and think that being a victim of abuse is their fault. I believe that in these situations the longer people hold themselves responsible for what horrible monsters in society do to them, they put their lives on hold.

So, how did I pull myself out of this? First of all, I had to talk about it. I had to get over my grief. I had to write about it. I put myself in counseling. I got into action. For so many years, I kept myself stuck. I had run from myself for so many years. Until I found this woman, that was a counselor and she had experienced what I had experienced, and she told me that I was stuck in a pattern. She told me her story and that what had happened was not my fault. I met with her for and a few other counselors for about a year. I found out there were tools that I could use. Much like in the rooms, I could pray about it, I could imagine getting my revenge. I know that sounds horrible. However, I had so much pent up anger and remorse. So, this tool helped me, because in my situation I never got closure. Which really helped me, because what had happened to me was hurting my relationship with that one person that I truly loved and that poor soul paid for what happened to me for years.

Today I don't have to continually relive what happened to me. Some days are better than others. Though, today I am truly blessed. The man I truly love has gone through some of the things that I went through and we are able to help each other. We have been friends for ten years. So, good things can come happen to those that think they will never find peace.

The big reason I got messed up was when I was messed up I didn't feel any emotions. I didn't have the thoughts that I wasn't good enough. When I was loaded I didn't have a tarnished self-esteem. I got loaded and stayed loaded because I didn't have living skills and my life was unmanageable.

So, when I went off to college, after high school, I was just running away from home. I didn't have the skills to be successful. I continued my drinking and it got way out of control and I found there was things in the world that made me fell better than alcohol made me feel. Meaning I continued partying and was introduced to uppers and what I thought at the time was fun to do. I didn't see anything wrong with these things as everyone else was doing it. So, I didn't last long in college as my parents quickly caught on to what I was doing and I had to go back home and enter into junior college.

Consequences

...

I was very upset about this. I got into a lot of trouble and had to pay a lot of consequences behind this. For the very first time I was paying consequences of having to pay my parents back financially. Which luckily for me, I just went back to working at Walmart.

Though paying back my parents money really didn't stop me with my partying. I just paid my parents back and started going to clubs. I just continued to hang around with the wrong people. I continued to make the wrong decisions. I had been diagnosed as having depression and possibly bipolar disorder. Though, at the time I didn't want any help, I didn't think I needed any help. I had to sink all the way to the bottom until I was teachable. It took me a long time to become willing. As when I was drinking and everything, everything was everyone else's fault. It took me a long while to see that I created my own problems and that no one was making me drink. As, I still had an excuse for everything.

I later went back to college trying to take some classes. It didn't go the way I wanted it to go. Though, I met some decent people finally. These people were able to help me see that my attitude and perspective were off course.

So, I went back home for a little while as my mom was really sick and I finally cared. I finally saw things for what they were. I saw that I was addicted to everything. I saw that my mom was dying from the stress of the insanity and the hard life she chose to live. So, I hung around and did what I could to help out. I helped her out until I went on with my life. As, she and I constantly argued and the family sure knew what was best. So, I went back to school and moved with my boyfriend. The funny thing with me was that I would party hardcore for a while and then I would get tired of it and quit for a while. So, after quitting for about four months we had thought I was done with the insanity. Until I started doing the old behavior and feeling guilty and I started drinking again.

Unmanageability

...

I want to make sure that those reading this understand that my life was totally and completely unmanageable. There are people today that still will not talk to me because of the wreckage of my past. Some of which I still cannot remember why these people quite literally hate me. The rooms of recovery in my early recovery were the only place I had attended that asked me to keep coming back. As the pattern I was used to being told to never call again or to stay away for good.

The one thing about my wreckage of my past that I hate is that I have lost a lot of time being miserable when I really didn't have to be like that. I lost time that I could have been with my mother before she passed away. In my addiction I lost a lot of time that I could have been bettering myself. However, I will never get that time back. Which is hurtful, however, today I know that provided I stay sober and do the right thing, I will not have to pay the kinds of consequences I had to pay in early recovery.

Mental Health

• • •

One thing I want to discuss in this book is mental health. I want to make sure that people understand that those with mental illness or emotional problems do have a place in recovery. There is a twelve-step program that helps a lot of people called Dual Recovery, mental health addiction. Emotions Anonymous is another common name for this. There is a lot of literature out there on this subject. Please look into the Twelve Promises of Emotions Anonymous. This anonymous program is very helpful. It allows people to understand their diagnosis, learn to cope, and it gives you tools for living.

If you are in the Emotions Anonymous program and you go to AA meetings or NA meetings, please use caution. As unfortunately the different anonymous programs have their own beliefs, and sponsors are not doctors nor are members doctors. The reason I put this disclaimer here is I have seen many members of AA and NA come to AA or NA before attending emotions anonymous or outside help and they relapse due to sponsors or other alcoholics/addicts telling them they are not sober or clean because they take medications.

Many people in NA or AA do not understand that certain people must be on certain medications due to severe depression, suicide, mania or other very serious life or death medical situations. Thus, please use caution, and find someone that understands mental illness if you are looking for sponsorship or step work in the AA or NA communities.

I don't want to give the wrong perspective, as I love AA and NA. Its just due to the journey that I had, I would like to let people know that there are some pitfalls and ruts out there. It is a very common thing in the rooms to have dual diagnosis and there is hope provided it is dealt with accordingly.

Sponsorship

...

Next, I would like to talk about sponsorship, as it is a very important to recovery. Without sponsorship, there is no recovery for the struggling alcoholic/addict. As, one person helping another is really the big deal. Sponsorship is not rocket science. What sponsorship is to me is having someone walk you through the steps and someone that is there to help the newcomer or the old-timer. If you are new in the program, please do not think you are wasting a sponsor's time as sponsorship helps the sponsor as much as the sponsee.

I have had many a situation where my sponsees helped me just as much as I was helping them. The reason I say this is that the support group is very important in recovery. As there are times when my sponsor is just not available and if I am feeling like drinking or whatever at the time, having someone in recovery that understands recovery is especially important. As the support group helps many individuals stay sober.

If you are new to the program the suggestions that have worked for me are to go to meetings, have a support group, have a phone list, sponsorship, step work, and service work. This may appear as a lot of work. However, if you are a woman, get with the women. If you are a man work with the men. This appears "cheesy". However, newcomers do not need to be mingling with the opposite sex as relationships in early recovery quickly become resentments.

Relationships

...

So, onto relationships; I am not suggesting that people that are married to divorce. I am not saying I have all the answers. However in my experience, typically people new in recovery meet coeds in recovery. The idea that I am trying to hit home with readers is that a relationship in early recovery is typically two people in recovery that hardly know how to stay sober. So, they rush into a relationship, and generally both parties are hurt, one or both relapse and have a sour taste in their mouth for recovery.

The thing that I am trying to explain to people is that most people prior to recovery do not have healthy relationships. So, two people in recovery that get together typically have a lot of issues that that have quick solutions provided they do what is suggested. However, by getting into a relationship, with two alcoholics/addicts involved is not a good idea because you are setting yourself up for failure, heart ache, resentments and possibly relapse.

I do want to explain quickly that there are people out there that are in relationships with two alcoholics/addicts involved that do well. However, I recommend that in the first year people do not make any major changes. As I like to be able to work with my sponsees genuinely so they have tools, and so they work on themselves and are ok with themselves. Meaning that I like my sponsees to have the building blocks so when good or bad things happen that are out of their comfort zone they don't immediately give up and relapse.

My Relapse

...

As in my experience, I had nine months clean and relapsed over a broken heart. Which made my recovery in my opinion more challenging as I thought at the beginning of coming back to the program that I knew something about recovery. When I had relapsed so I had no understanding because if I knew how to stay sober, why did I relapse.

The reason I relapsed was that life didn't go as I had planned. I was hungry, angry, lonely and tired. Which, I have to really watch out for in my program. The reason I explained this is that when I have these feelings I need to address them. When I was in my addiction, I never felt emotions. I thought that emotions were angry, happy, love, hate, and simply extremes of emotions. I have truly learned a lot in recovery.

As, I have a lot more emotions today and today I simply walk through my emotions. It is important for me to feel my emotions and move on. Instead of running from my emotions or getting loaded behind my emotions. Today, feelings are not road maps. Meaning I don't have to react to peoples emotions or bad attitudes. I can just smile and get on with my day. I do not have to act out just because it's the easy thing to do.

Now, I would like to move on to some other stories that I would like to discuss. The next couple of stories are about women in recovery. I like both men and women's stories.

However, the reason I like to zero in on women's stories is in my experience there are not a lot of women in recovery. The meetings I go to there are very little women that attend and there are fewer young people in recovery.

Stories, You Too Can Recover

...

I have had the privilege to work with a twenty year old that is very close to home for me. Her story is that she was drinking and drugging for about five or six years. She was running away from home, staying in hotel rooms, running with criminals, and for the most part hanging with dangerous people. Thus, the fact is this is a program of living and dying. Well, she hit a few bottoms. Some legal problems popped up for her. Then, one night she went out and got in a lot of trouble. She went out with her friends and they were drinking and driving and it was raining and the weather was bad. Some bad decisions ended her up with a rolled SUV and her friend expelled from the vehicle. She ended up with some jail time and some serious changes that had to happen. Today three years later she has a little over a year of sobriety. She is a lady today. Which in her past, many people would have been saying she wouldn't last much longer. As people who live on the run for a long period of time don't make it. As, she was running from one family or friends place to another. She didn't stay more than a day with anyone. Though today, she is a productive member of society. She is sharing the message and for someone like that to have a decent understanding of the steps. She has had her ups and downs. However, this is a beautiful story if you ask me.

I have another friend in recovery that I help out on a regular basis. She is about in her forties. She has grown kids, a home, her life is not perfect, and she has a lot of living problems. I haven't sponsored anyone that doesn't have problems with living life on life's terms.

However, today she has a little over a year sober. When I met this woman and she asked me to sponsor her, I never thought she had a chance. As the state and probation department were seriously asking her to do a lot of things. She was in outpatient, which in our county is a very challenging counseling group to stay in because in that clinic less than five percent stay sober for more than four or five months. She also had a lot of fines to pay to the state. Not to mention the only job she had held outside of selling drugs was working in fast food. So, she didn't have much for skills when the state was telling her to find a job and they wanted her to be employed for a long period of time. Today she doesn't make a lot of money, but she makes enough to pay the bills that she has. For the most part she is happy.

She is physically and mentally disabled. However, she works through that and the chronic pain and she works hard. Every day is a challenge for her. If someone like her and myself can stay sober anyone has a chance as recovery is for people who want it not people who need it as recovery is about action. The people that I see in the rooms that make recovery a part of their lives typically stay around.

Those that sit on the fence not knowing whether they want recovery or relapse typically relapse. Another woman that I know has had a lot of battles. She has nine years of recovery. She is married to an alcoholic and she and her husband both have nine years of sobriety. The things that she does to stay sober are she works with the local woman's shelter and helps newcomers a lot. She stays engaged. She doesn't just show up at one group all of the time. She has a support group and she stays busy. Her life isn't all roses as she has lost jobs, she has struggled a lot academically and she always seems to have curve balls thrown in her way.

The thing that I have learned from her is that she stays in today and that she has decided that she will stay sober no matter what. For me that was a very hard thing to understand. Staying sober no matter what.

As, with a lot of others and myself, I have spoken with I had an excuse for each time I used. I got in an argument with someone, I lost money, I got a job, I lost a job, I got a new home, I was evicted, or it was the holidays, etc. I am so blessed that I have had the opportunity to work with some of these people that I have been able to learn something from. Not to mention each and every person in my support group has helped me grow or learn something new about recovery.

I know another person in recovery, which has a year clean. If you ever met this person, you would think he has been around for at least ten years. He just acts right and dresses right. Which shows me that I should not make quick decisions regarding others in recovery. He has two children and a sweet family, which he attributes to recovery. This man is "Mr. Recovery". The reason I say that is every time I see him he has a smile on his face, and he is always doing service work. He truly understands the concept of if you don't have recovery you have nothing. The funny thing is when I first met this individual I immediately thought he had it going on. When in reality he is just like myself, just another person in recovery trying to do better.

I know in my early recovery, I would have never imagined the things that I have gone through sober. In the beginning I could not see myself sober for a week, a month or a year. I have dealt with a lot of challenging things in recovery. Such as death, loss, resentments, jealousy, family members being challenging to deal with, changes from one sponsor to another, sponsees relapsing, working, health problems and sometimes just wrestling with being a productive member of society.

One of the things that were really important for me to understand early in recovery is that I am not below or above the people at the meetings that I attend. I will not give the name of the group I attend. However, there are a lot of hard-core drug addicts. Today, I understand that I too, could go to these lengths to get or stay high.

I believe that if I were to pick up I would start where I left off and go into an even darker chapter of alcoholism and addiction. The reason I refer to my addiction as alcoholism and addiction is that for this addict I have a lot of patterns and avenues of addiction. Typically when my addiction creeps up I will start drinking and I think I have my alcoholism under control, and once I have this "concept", my alcoholism spirals out of control and before I know it the cycle of my addiction has begun. I don't do anything without drinking and before I know it I am doing gateway drugs that are smoked and within a short period of time I look for and find my drug of choice.

I really don't want to concentrate this book on what my drug of choice is. (As, my drug of choice depends on what day of the week it is, and whatever is either put on the table or easily accessible.) The only reason I have talked about my experience is so that those that pick up this book don't think I have no experience.

Guilt, Shame and Forgiveness

. . .

A topic that is really important to me is guilt and shame and forgiveness of self. For a long time, when I worked the twelve steps, I would forget to forgive myself. I had this concept that the things I had done in my life were horrible things when the things that I thought were so horrible were just little things.

Simple things like standing people up, or not putting a two-week notice at a job. I was never perfect when I was in my addiction, but don't you know, I came into the program and immediately thought I had to work a perfect program. I would get with a particular sponsor and they didn't have time for me, or I would find out they weren't working the steps so I would move on and find another sponsor and I would feel guilty over stupid things like that.

When I got to the program, I had this concept that everything that happened was my fault whether it was positive or negative things. I would get into a argument with a family member or friend and have to immediately admit I was wrong, whether it was just a situation where we had different opinions or ideas or whether I was being mean and not fighting fair.

In my home, we seriously try to have some simple ground rules. I do not allow for anyone under any conditions to drink and or do drugs in my home. As my home is my sanctuary and it has to be an atmosphere of safety, recovery, and not complete chaos. We have some simple rules and I will admit they are not always followed. However, we do make an effort. No one is allowed to kick any member of the home out, under any circumstances. We do our best to sit down and discuss our challenges with each other. That way if someone constantly does a behavior that really bothers another individual there is an opportunity to have that behavior changed and or discussed.

Fighting Fair

...

Here are some simple ideas as to fighting fair. I highly recommend conflict resolution not in the middle of heightened emotions or feelings. Having a yelling, screaming match or physical altercation rarely solves any problem (s). Thus, the first common suggestion is to remain calm, do try not to react excessively involving challenging situations. By staying calm, it is more likely that others will hear your viewpoint.

Another very important thing is to express emotions in words as opposed to actions. Sitting down and speaking about the challenge with   someone directly and honestly about how you feel can be a very powerful form of communication. Do make sure that if you begin to feel anger or rage, step away from the situation, and take a walk or whatever is necessary to avoid an argument where unnecessary words or arguments occur. As, in the midst of anger and acting out on feelings typically does not solve problems. Remember you are problem solving and saying things you do not mean just ads to the chaos not problem solving. When you are sitting down and discussing whatever happened that was offensive or said, make sure to be direct and to the point. If the individual or individuals involved are not told exactly what happened it makes it much harder for them to fix the problem.

Make sure to deal with one issue at a time. As if you simply just are telling each other everything that is offensive and its along list and you just dump a long list on each other this just causes a argument as opposed to sitting down and coming up with solutions. Make sure that when everyone sits down everyone understands that attacking areas of personal sensitivity only offers an atmosphere of distrust, anger and vulnerability, which is not conductive to finding a solution. Make sure that everyone involved needs to avoid accusations. As accusations simply cause others to be defensive. Instead discuss how someone's actions made you feeling. Make sure generalization is avoided and words like never and always are avoided, as these are typically inaccurate and only heighten tension. Do avoid exaggerating or inventing a complaint or going around your feelings about it as this prevents the real issues surfacing. Simply stick with the facts and honest feelings.

Another thing I hear a lot of in the rooms is storing up resentments. Storing up a number of grievances and hurt feelings over time as this is counterproductive. It is best to deal with problems as they present themselves, instead of stuffing "problems" and then people just blow up. Make sure that all parties are listening and involved or you may have to stop and try again later. One of the big things that I find very important is to establish common ground rules. It is really important to make sure that all parties involved understand the ground rules.

In order to make the Fair Fighting ground rules effective in resolving a specific conflict, use the following steps:

Step One: Do not begin until you ask yourself, "What exactly is bothering me? What do I want the other person to do or not do? Are my feelings proportionate to the issue?"

Step two: Know and understand what your goals and or objectives are before you begin. What are some of the possible outcomes that could be acceptable to you?

Step three: Keep in mind and recall that the plan is not to "win" but to come to a mutually satisfying and peaceful solution to the problem.

Step four: Set a time for a discussion with the partner-in-conflict. It should be as soon as possible but agreeable to both persons. Springing something when another is unprepared may leave the other person feeling that he or she has to fend off an attack. If you encounter resistance to setting a time, try to help the other person see that the problem is important to you.

Step five: State the problem clearly and concisely. At first, try to stick to the facts. Then, once you've stated the facts, state your feelings. Use "I" messages to describe feelings of anger, hurt, or disappointment. Avoid "you" messages such as "you make me angry...."

Step six: Invite your partner-in-conflict to share his or her point of view, and use active listening skills. Take care not to interrupt, and genuinely try to hear his or her concerns and feelings. If it seems helpful, try to restate what you have heard in a way that lets your partner know you have completely understood, and ask your partner to do the same for you.

Step seven: Try to take the other's perspective - that is, attempt to see the problem through his or her eyes. The "opposing" viewpoint can make sense even if you differ in opinions.

Step eight: Offer specific solutions, and invite the other person to offer solutions, also.

Step nine: Discuss the pros and cons of each proposal.

Step ten: Be ready find some middle ground. Allowing the other person only one option will likely delay resolution. Set a trial period (actual time period) for the new behavior. At the end of the trial period, you can chat about the possibility of modifying or continuing the change. If no solution has been reached regarding the original problem, do try again.

What Would I Like to Receive From My Recovery?

...

For me, I have had to use the K.I.S.S. formula regarding my recovery. As in my humble opinion recovery is a simple process. If I get up in the morning and pray, pray continually throughout the day, read the literature, hang with the winners, go to meetings, use my support group, talk to people on the phone and invite them to group functions, and make these components a regular part of my life I have a chance in staying clean and sober one more day.

I remember when I was new to the rooms and my sponsor told me to write down what I wanted out of recovery. I wrote stability, friends, family, happiness, etc. If I had only known earlier in life what could be possible from working some steps and going to meetings and putting some action into this program. However it takes time and I had to truly want this deal.

The Pitfalls

...

For myself, I have noticed there are a few pitfalls I have to watch out for. If I stay away from the program for just a week, I forget where I come from, I forget I have problems with substance abuse, and I forget that I have to take medications, and rapidly if I don't catch myself, I end up in either one of two places, in the hospital and or relapsing.

This dual diagnosis that I deal with means I have more than one item to address and if I don't address these, the diseases let me know. Which means I have to continue to work the steps. I understand that reading the twelve steps and the twelve traditions sometimes appears that individuals simply work the twelve steps once and all will be well.

Not to mention, in my experience, attending other twelve step programs is helpful. I do not mean at all to go get involved in other fellowships and stay away from your normal meetings and such. I am merely suggesting that after attending AA or whatever anonymous works for you, the alcoholic or addict may find out you have more than one addiction.

Those With Mental Illness Can Recovery Too

. . .

The reason I am harping on my dual diagnosis is that I want people to walk away from this book provided the shoe fits understanding that people with dual diagnosis can have "normal" lives. (Meaning people that are productive members of society) It is just that those with dual diagnosis need do incredible amounts of action. The item that allowed me to understand this disease was by asking friend of mine about my behavior, and journaling my disease. (Meaning rating it on a daily basis on extremes and seeing if there were trends) Such as, I have a friend that was a roommate of mine for a short time and she also has a mother that is bipolar. I asked her if during certain times of the day I was more depressed or manic and I asked her about if I eat or drink anything that seemed to change the trends. (Such as eating candy, soda, or taking pain medication like aspirin)

As I have noted that the more caffeine I drink makes me more irritated. I also found out that I don't do things that increase the effectiveness of the medication that I take. Which is something I will have to work on one day at a time, as some days are better than others. As, it is Progress not perfection.

The thing that has been really working these days is that psychiatry and psychology hand in hand seem to make things better. I won't lie that I just run right out and sign myself up, as I don't like to go to meetings or appointments. It's just that over the years, I have found certain things effective, so I would rather just go and not want to than the alternative, which is relapse. When I say relapse, in this sense, it usually entails hospitalization and for me, this is usually long term. So, I would rather be honest with my doctors and therapists then end up locked up in hospitals, etc. The thing that is really helpful is to have doctors and therapists that look at the whole picture before getting into the therapy.

The other thing that I like to stress is that if you have the diseases that I do. These diseases will ruin every avenue of your life. Shopping addiction, Spiritually, Relationships, legal problems and the list goes on and it just festers until the individual does something to take care of it.

Finding the Right Medication

. . .

I wish I could say that it didn't take me a while to find the right medication that worked for me. However, it was a long ten years. I was very sick for a long time. The journey had nothing to do with me, as I was totally insane going from doctor to doctor. It ruined my credit report. I was always broke, had no money.

Though, something kept me going. I kept praying to god that something would come up, and I just kept praying that something would happen. (PUSH pray until something happens) I finally found this doctor in Abilene Texas. I am sure he doesn't practice any more. What I had to go to see that doctor. A friend of mine was a psychologist and she just handed me lists and lists of doctors and she had highlighted the ones she had heard good things about. So, out of desperation I went to this doctor's office. I showed up at eight am and sat there until they closed. I did not have an appointment, but I was determined to get a appointment with this doctor as I knew he had a full list of patients. Finally at the end of the day, this nurse noticed I was still trying to get the secretary to get me an appointment. She and the secretary went round and round about this as the nurse had seen that I was there all day. So the nurse took my information and she gave me an appointment to see the doctor and get on his list .Due to this doctor being a specialist in psychiatry and he was good at what he did, it was a miracle that this nurse got me an appointment to get right into that office. At that time, I found out the one medication worked. It wasn't the complete treatment that worked for me, as at the time I was too young and I wasn't interested in doing my part. However, it was a beginning point in my getting better.

Asking For Help

...

Today, I have a very good doctor and things are looking good. However, that is because I ask for help and I happen to have some luck. I truly believe its because I am truthful with my doctor, and I don't play around with my health today. Today, I genuinely want to stay well and am willing to go to any length. As today my health is important to me.

Going to any length. That is an important key to my recovery and my program. In my relapses and addiction, I went to any length to get my drug of choice. So, today in my recovery, I have to go to any length to work the steps and keep what I have today.

The Question Most Commonly Asked: How does one get sober, what is the process?

...

This is a powerful question. As, people are very different. What works for most people may not work for some. What worked for me may not work for the next person. However I can address what works for most alcoholics/addicts. For most people, rehab works. However, the biggest misconception with recovery is that you go to rehab and you are good to go. Recovery is a lifetime membership provided one wants to recover and stay in recovery. A lot of people think they go to rehab and that is it. I wish I could say that all people dealing with recovery just go to rehab and they have a great life. If it were that easy then I wouldn't know people that have gone to thirty different rehabs.

Some other videos that are helpful are 28 days starring Sandra Bullock, My Name is Bill W, and Clean and Sober starring Michael Keaton. The reason I have listed those is that these are very good for family members, and anyone dealing with alcoholism, Alanon or any other similar item.

Recovery is a very challenging thing. It is said that it is a simple program for complicated people. However, there are many things that come up when the alcoholic/addict overcomes the cravings and are given a daily reprieve from their old way of life. As, once this occurs most people in recovery find out they have other addictions not limited to gambling, shopping addictions, relationship problems and other items that require counseling, and other forms of outside help.

AA was the first twelve-step program and was the source and has been the model for all similar recovery groups such as Gamblers Anonymous, Emotions Anonymous, Narcotics Anonymous, Sexaholics Anonymous, Sex Addicts Anonymous, Overeaters Anonymous, and Al-Anon/Alateen, among others. I just wanted to let people understand that in my opinion everyone in society is recovering from something.

Whether it is violence, abuse, alcoholism, addiction, emotional problems or physical challenges. In our fast paced lives, to be human means you are dealing with something.

At this point, I would like to discuss working the steps. Working the steps is a very important component to staying sober. I wish merely going to meetings would keep people sober for long amounts of time. I really don't like to hear people say that recovery is easy. The reason I shy away from this is that recovery is not easy. It can become a habit. The reason I say that recovery is not easy is that to be in recovery means to be doing the abnormal, the uncomfortable.

Another thing is that simply working steps for an hour a week or an hour a month is simply a beginning point. As, I learn the steps and then I have to work on fitting them into my life. Also, a mistake I got into when I first came in was that I thought the steps were all there were.

I start my sponsees off on the literature. I am so blessed that I get to work with a lot of spanking new people. At first I was like what can I offer these women? Then it came to me, I offer them what I have been offered. So, really the beginning is not the steps.

The beginning is stopping and staying stopped. Then, you learn the information in the literature. You do all of this with the help of a sponsor, a sponsor that has a sponsor to be more specific. There is no reason to waste time self-sponsoring as that is just a copout.

Meaning, I come in and I become teachable and I get with someone with quality sobriety. As a lot of people come in and concentrate on finding someone with a certain amount of time. Having time in the rooms is important but having time and having something to offer is a bit more important in my understanding.

As, I went through a lot of sponsors in the beginning as some of them seemed to need the program more than I did. As, I truly believe that some are sicker than others and some recover at different rates.

Another thing about sponsorship is that a sponsor isn't something someone should do just because a rehab facility requires it. If I had a dollar for everyone that has asked me for my number and to help them I would be rich by now.

As, I don't sponsor anyone that isn't ready. As some simply are not ready yet. Some are doing more "research" on a relapse. As recovery and relapse are choices we have in recovery. These are active decisions in recovery that people make. If you want to stay in recovery you cant just hang around and hold the walls up, you have to get involved, get to know people, and learn about what recovery is, the bottom line…. What are you willing to do for your recovery today? My experience is that I went to any length to get loaded, am I willing to go to any length for my recovery?

As for the steps, these allow people to see results in their lives. It is awesome to see people that want what another person has and to see the love of the program working in people's lives. As, first they have to listen and then, they finally hear someone that shares exactly what they are going through and then these two men or women start working together is truly a miracle. This program works as long as you stay in action and continue to work the steps.

As far as I am concerned, the first step is the most important step. Well, the real first step is quitting the addiction. Then, we work the first step, which is the only step that I see that people need to work thoroughly. If I have any reservations, I need to look at them in the first step. As I had to grab a hold of the idea that I am an addict and my life is unmanageable and there is absolutely no reason for me to pick up today.

No matter what happens I have made the decision not to get loaded or whatever today. There is nothing that can happen to me that is worth loosing my joy as anything can be worked out in recovery.

I have found that my understanding of the program and how I stay sober and that I have to continue my recovery even after I have worked the twelve steps. The idea is not to just work the twelve steps and stop. I have probably worked the twelve steps completely at least ten times. It is also important that I do service work also.

Now this doesn't mean I have to grab every newcomer that walks through the door and I have to compromise my recovery and be superwoman in the area of recovery. This simply means I don't get complacent.

In my experience this means just doing little things. What I am getting at is to stay in action. If you are sponsoring, it means you are working steps yourself. Sometimes, its simple things like making yourself available, answering your phone, and talking to another person in the program, or simply lending another person a hand.

This doesn't mean you compromise your recovery and you move in every sorry person that you meet. As people will use you as a doormat if you are not careful which is why I say boundaries are important. Boundaries are not talked about much in the rooms but they have been important in my recovery as I am a pushover and sometimes I don't see it when I am being taken advantage of. Boundaries are not just telling someone what you will and will not tolerate. It means letting the person know what you will and will not tolerate and what the consequences will be.

In my experience, I was used to getting loaded every day. For me, it wasn't a once in a while thing. Which shows me that to stay in recovery, I have to put some action behind it. When the wreckage of my past was weighing on my shoulders like a ton of bricks, you bet I was at a meeting every night.

The thing is now that I have years without the consequences of using and all that negativity, it is very easy to forget where I come from. My sick mind tells me I don't need to go to meetings, that I can smoke one and nothing will happen, that I can have one drink and I won't relapse, and I have to watch myself with all the alcohol commercials out there. I can be having a great day, and notice a beer bottle on the ground and sometimes in a matter of minutes if I am not doing my "maintenance plan" I can find myself in the relapse isle of the grocery store. The disease of alcoholism and addiction is very innocent at times.

A big thing that I hear a lot about in the rooms is grief, and issues with the fourth step. To me, I couldn't forgive myself until I did a thorough fourth step. So, I will include my understanding of the fourth step.

In my experience, I have found that a thorough fourth step was the key to my being able to stop continually working step one through three and not going any further. It is highly recommended that one write out a list daily of ten positive things about yourself and a list of ten blessings in your life daily to help keep depression at bay.

Childhood

1. What kind of relationship did your mother have with her parents?

2. What kind of relationship did your father have with his parents?

3. Were you wanted at birth?

4. Write out the circumstances of your family at the time of your birth. Specifically:
   a. Family size
   b. Age differences (Your parents, brothers & sisters)
   c. Financial status
   d. Was there laughter?
   e. Arguing?
   f. Depression?
   g. Were other relatives living with you?
   h. Other circumstances?

5. In general, describe what you think your family thought of you.
   a. Did you feel your parents' attitude toward you was different than other parents toward their children?
   b. How old were you at the birth of brothers and sisters?
   c. How did you feel about the new arrivals?
   d. Were either of your parents sick enough to need hospitalizations?
   e. Were you separated from any important family member?
   f. Was there fear or guilt about this separation? (In other words, did you feel responsible?)

6. Were you threatened by the Boogey Man or the Devil if you misbehaved?
   a. If so, what were your fears in this regard?

7. A child is made to feel guilty about his/her normal sexual curiosity. This comes about by his/her being caught and punished for touching himself/herself, or being caught masturbating, or playing "Doctor", or for participating in group masturbation.

Many parents tell children that sexual feelings are evil and must be punished. With no sex education, and given this sort of teaching, a child will naturally distort whathe/she knows about sex. When a child is exposed to fully developed nude persons (For instance in the bathroom at home, or in public), he/she may begin to feel inadequacy in adult life, even after the person is a thoroughly developed adult.

    a. Write down any of the above experiences that you have had or make you feel uneasy.

8. Did you have a difficult time pleasing one or both of your parents?

    a. Were you constantly directed and redirected by your parents?

    b. Did you obey docilely?

    c. Did you have feelings of distress and boredom?

    d. Were you afraid of the dark?

    e. Were you afraid to fight?

    f. Or were you afraid not to fight because of pressure from your mother or father or older brothers or sisters or others?

9. Did your parents submit to your whims and immature demands most of the time?

    a. Did you have temper tantrums?

    b. How did your parents punish you? By trying to reason, or was it physical?

    c. How did you react to punishment?

10. What kind of marriage do you think your parents had?

    a. If they fought, did you resent it?

    b. Did it scare you?

    c. Were you used to breaking up their fights?

    d. Did you take one side or the other?

    e. Were your parents preoccupied with themselves?

    f. Did they lack awareness of your needs?

g. Was there an absence of affection, concern, or loving attention in your home?

11. If your parents were from different religions, did you feel confused about it?

a. What particular idea of "God" was impressed upon you?

b. Did you reject this concept because it seemed inadequate?

c. If you did reject this idea, did you imagine you had abandoned the God idea entirely?

d. Did your parents teach you that God was a loving God or a punishing God?

12. Were you afraid of storms?

13. List all the feelings of guilt, fear, resentments, you had toward each person in your life as a child (not your feelings now).

14. Did you feel you were "bad"?

a. Did you put yourself into situations that caused others to punish you?

15. List the first time that you ever stole anything?

a. Inventory all your childhood thefts.

16. How old were you when you first masturbated?

a. Were you ever caught and made to feel guilty?

b. Did you feel guilty even though you weren't caught?

c. What other kinds of sexual curiosity were you involved in (homosexual, animal, with any other members of the family, anything else)?

17. If you were named after someone, what was that person like?

18. Did your family move often?

a. If so, did you make friends and then have to break off the relationship so often that you became afraid to become close?

19. Do you remember starting school?

a. What were your feelings?

b. Try to remember each successive grade in school and as you do, write out the resentments you felt toward teachers, pupils, anyone.

c. Any fights?

d. Slights?

e. Hurts?

f. Embarrassments?

20. Did you resent your relatives, friends, or parents? If so, list them. No resentment is too small to mention.

21. What kind of language did your parents use?

a. Were you ashamed of them for this or anything else?

b. Did you ever see your parents in the nude?

c. What were your feelings?

d. Did you ever see or hear your parents having sex?

e. What were your feelings?

22. In every family, a child usually has certain "chores" assigned.

a. What were yours?

b. Were they fair?

c. Could you do them in ways that would please your parents?

d. Do you remember longing for a carefree childhood because of the absence of play?

23. Did your parents seem to like your friends better than they did you?

a. Did your friends seem to like your parents better than they did you?

b. If so, did you resent this?

24. Any bad experiences at Sunday school?

a. Or at summer camp?

25. Were you an only child?

a. Did you resent this or enjoy it?

26. Did your parents want a child of the opposite sex when they had you?

a. Did they name you, or dress you, to match their sex choice?

b. Did your appearance (looks, dress, etc.) embarrass you?

c. Did you feel you were "different" from your classmates?

27. Were you treated as a nuisance or a burden?

28. Did you treat possible friends with hostility or obnoxious behavior?

a. Did you force friends to abandon friendly behavior?

29. Did you feel your parents' attitude toward you was different than other parents toward their children?

Write down any other childhood memories that were painful.

Which of the above questions about childhood was the toughest for you to answer?

Do you know why?

End of Childhood Section

ADOLESCENCE

Often an adolescent relies on the misguided sex information obtained from his peers. This can produce a number of severe problems (i.e. never outgrowing the desire to have sex with the opposite parent, brother, sister...sometimes the desire for sexual activities with the parent of the same sex.) Although these are unconscious desires, they bring on conscious guilt's that have to be dealt with. Distortion may come when a person is too young emotionally to handle adult sex. There is involvement because of peer pressure or the desire to please another. Not being in touch with adult feelings, pretenses set up which then leads to anger, disappointment, and guilt. These feelings, in turn, can have a tendency to prevent normal sexual and emotional growth. The guilt prevents the person from talking the feelings out with a mature adult, which may result in a need to repeat the same pattern over and over again.

1. Write down your experience concerning the above, both heterosexual and homosexual.

2. Some girls are taught that men are interested in sex only, and some boys are taught that they must be "the greatest of all time." These attitudes are destructive and damaging to the total person.
    a. Have you experienced either of these attitudes?
    b. Is there a pattern?
    c. How has it affected you?

3. Did you have friends when you were an adolescent?

4. Did you consider friendly overtures a possible trick?

5. Did you have feelings of complete worthlessness?

6. What kind of friend were you?

7. What interest or lack of interest did you have in school?

8. How was your social life?

9. Did you participate in sports or creative activities such as music, art, etc.?

10. What were the reasons for your participation or non-participation in these activities?

11. Were you a troublemaker? If so, in what way?
    a. Did you destroy property?
    b. Did you resent leaders-either physical or mental?
    c. Did what seemed to satisfy others provide no satisfaction for you?
    d. Did you tend to drift, lack initiative, be short on persistence?
    e. Did you feel passive discontent?
    f. Did you resent not being the most handsome or beautiful person at school?

12. Did you feel you were a coward because you didn't want to fight?
    a. Of did you like to fight?
    b. Were you a bully?
    c. If you are a boy, did you feel embarrassed because boys made fun of you or girls avoided you?
    d. If you are a girl, did you feel embarrassed because girls made fun of you or boys avoided you?
    e. Were you very sensitive to rebuff and almost automatically hostile?

13. Did you have a difficult time pleasing yourself?
    a. Did it bother you if you made mistakes?
    b. Were you overly concerned with every detail?

14. Some people feel inadequate as adults because they were at one time exposed to youngsters more developed at that time. Were you exposed to other children in gym class or the restrooms who were older than you and more developed physically?
    a. How did you feel then?
    b. How do you feel now?

15. Did you drift in and out of relationships?

16. Did you suffer intensely from insecurities and tend to keep people at a distance?

17. Did you feel that deep down you lacked an identity of your own?

18. Did you resent not being part of a crowd?
    a. Or not being a leader?
    b. Or not being "in"?

19. Were you shy or outgoing?
    a. How are you now?

20. Does any particular type of person make you shy?

21. If you dropped out of school explain your feelings and reasons?

22. Anything happen to you in high school that was a continuing source of shame?

23. Did your parents compare you to other family members or friends?

a. Did you resent them for wanting you to be like someone else?

24. How did you get the attention of your family?

25. Did you have great longings for someone to care for you?

a. Did you make an effort to appear self-sufficient, independent of others,
detached, aloof?

b. Did you pout, sulk, be a good child, have temper tantrums, act like a
dummy?

26. Do you remember the kind of lies you told (if any)?

a. How did you feel when you got caught lying?

27. What was the most embarrassing incident of your adolescence?

a. Are there any others that you remember?

28. Did you have great difficulty in giving or receiving love and affection?

29. If sexual feeling were discounted and "put down" in your family, there is a strong possibility that you will feel guilty about them. We "catch" attitudes. A boy who's pushed to always do better, or is criticized no matter what he does, may find himself having trouble in his sexual performance as an adult. Or a girl who has been told that it is not-okay to feel sexy may grow up to dislike her own body and distrust her feelings. These attitudes create unnatural or uncomfortable sexual behavior.

a. Did you "catch" any of these attitudes?

b. Can you see such attitudes cropping up in your life now?

c. First sexual intercourse:

    1. What were your feelings?

    2. Did you feel guilty?

    3. Did you feel disappointed?

    4. Be as explicit about the feelings as you can.

30. List in detail any homosexual experience, masturbation fantasy, or other sexual activity that you remember from this time. Keep in mind that we are not concerned about "with whom" or "on what date" or "how often"...rather, we are concerned about how you felt about the experience.

31. Did you get someone pregnant?

a. Or become pregnant yourself?

b. What did you do and how did you feel about your actions?

32. Were you ashamed of your parents?

a. Were they too old, too fat, too sloppy, too drunk, etc.?

b. Too whatever?

33. Did you have the kind of clothes that other kids wore?

34. Did you give the spiritual side of life a fair hearing?

a. Did you choose to believe that your human intelligence is the last word?

35. Was there enough money for the things that you needed?

a. If not, were you resentful that there wasn't?

b. If there was, did you take it too much for granted?

c. Did you feel any brothers or sisters got more than you did?

d. Write out your feelings about money as an adolescent.

e. Did you tend to be impulsive?

36. Did you tend to dominate some or many aspects of your life?

37. Were you the kind of child you would want to have?

38. Were you a thief?

39. Were you ever double-promoted (skipped a grade)?
    a. If so, did you have trouble catching-up emotionally?
    b. Were you held back a grade?
    c. How did you act?
    d. How did you feel...did you feel uncomfortable because you were younger,
older, than the other students?

40. Were you undependable as a friend...breaking off relationships without any explanation when someone or something who seemed better came along?

41. Did you pit one member of your family against another?

42. What was the best experience you had during this period of your life?
    a. The worst?

We've covered a lot of ground on these questions. Now, is there anything that made you particularly uncomfortable when writing about it? Have you put down everything that you can remember now that bugged you then? Even the simplest, most nit-picking things are important if they trouble you. Put them down now.

End of Adolescence Section

ADULTHOOD

1. Are you afraid of getting too close to another person for fear of being rejected?

2. Do you test your relationships repeatedly, looking for slights or any indifference in order to find some ground for complaint?

3. Do you reject others before they can reject you?

4. Are you so thin-skinned that you have trouble admitting any human weaknesses?

    a. List some of your weaknesses that you are able to accept.

    b. How well do you accept yourself in your own humanness?

    c. Are you able to be less defensive about these weaknesses?

5. Define Love.

    a. What do you feel it is?

    b. Do you drift in and out of relationships?

    c. Does it seem that people mean little to you?

    d. Do you feel the desire for mothering/fathering?

    e. For active caring?

    f. For unlimited acceptance?

6. If you are married or have been married... list the things you and your mate had in common and what your goals were at the onset of your marriage.

    a. If you have been married more than once, do this with each marriage.

    b. Now list the things that were different between you.

7. If you married a cold, unloving person, ask yourself why you chose that one to be your mate?

    a. Did you use it as an excuse to find new romances?

    b. Was your mother or father cold and unloving...and is this your chance to get even with them through your spouse?

8. Why did you get married?

    a. Or...why haven't you gotten married?

    b. Was the marriage for the right reasons?

    c. Did you marry earlier than your peer group?

    d. Later?

    e. Do you accept or resent the responsibilities of marriage and family?

    f. Do you share in the responsibilities for the families' problems?

9. Are you able to be cheerful when everything seems to be leading to despair?

10. Do you resist the impulse to complain to others about your situation?

    a. Are you able to forgive those who have injured you?

11. Do you continue to assume excessive responsibility if there is no longer afinancial need?

12. Do you allow your family to come between you and your spouse?

13. Do you make excessive demands and expectations of your spouse?

14. Are you able to admit that you have no authority or power over any other human being?

15. Do you create a pleasant, cheerful environment?
    a. Do you try to?

16. Do you feel all human beings are basically good and sensitive?

17. Are you still a baby in your parent's eyes and take advantage of it?
    a. Do you resent it?

18. Are you a baby in the eyes of your spouse?
    a. Do you resent it?

19. Do you infringe on the rights and dignity of others?

20. Have your parents gotten you out of trouble you should have been able to handle
by yourself?

21. Do you gossip about others?

22. Are you comfortable with someone who is less fortunate than you?

23. Do you know how to respond to the needs of others?
    a. To give of yourself?

24. When, and how, and in just what instances did your selfish pursuit of sex relations
damage other people and yourself?
    a. What people were hurt?
    b. How badly?
    c. Did you spoil your marriage and injure your children?
    d. Did you jeopardize your job or your standing in the community?

e. Just how did you react to these situations at the time?

f. Did you burn with guilt that nothing could extinguish?

g. Did you have bouts of depression?

h. Or did you insist that you were the pursued and not the pursuer...and thus absolve yourself?

25. How have you reacted to frustration in sexual matters?

a. When denied, have you become vengeful or depressed?

b. Did you "take it out" on other people?

c. If there was rejection or coldness in your home, did you use this as a reason for promiscuity?

d. Did you tend to be promiscuous with little or no lasting satisfaction or emotional interchange?

26. Many people who are lonely and don't really know how to love get involved senselessly in "sexcapades." The temporary loss of loneliness makes one call sex "love," but when the sexual partner is gone, it makes for an even greater feeling of loneliness.

a. Have you ever experienced this?

27. Are laws made for other people?

a. Do you make up your own laws as you go along?

28. If revenge were possible right now, who would be the top people on your list?

a. Why?

29. What are your present feelings about sex, parents, brothers, sisters, grandparents, friends, your children, your mate, your intimate friends, your job, on being a compulsive person, finances, divorce or marriage (depending on your present status)?

30. What are your hopes and goals?

31. Does diversion and distraction interfere with your adult goals?

    a. Do you believe that your situation is not really hopeless, and that you are
capable of improving it?

    b. Are you able to feel that tomorrow will be brighter if you've had a bad day?

32. Do you use sex as a punishment or a reward?

33. How much time do you spend with your family?

    a. With the program?

34. What is your greatest fear?

35. What is your sex life like?

    a. Is it as mature as you might want it to be?

    b. Are you disappointed in your mate for not fulfilling your sexual needs?

    c. Are you careless of your partner's feelings?

    d. Write out your ideal of a healthy sex life.

36. Do you engage in sex in order to build your own ego by a feeling of conquest?

37. Are you afraid of being sexually rejected?

38. Are you ashamed of your body or the way you look?

    a. Write out what's wrong with the physical you.

    b. Write out the best things about you physically.

    c. Now write out the things about yourself that you are ashamed of.

39. Do you feel you are still trying to please your parents?

40. Do you drive yourself to the point of exhaustion?

41. Do you accept that you can only do your best?

42. Do you use people to get what you want?

43. Do you expect others to pour out love, affection, and services?

44. Do you gossip or perform "character assassination" on others in order to "make it" in the business or social world?

    a. Or do you do this in an effort to feel superior (to the one gossiped about)?

45. If you are a thief, what have you stolen?

    a. Don't forget to include employer's time and the good feelings others had
and you destroyed.

    b. Have you used your employer's facilities, supplies or equipment for your
personal use without permission?

46. Do you have a pattern of getting sick?

    a. Do you go to doctors repeatedly without finding anything organically
wrong?

    b. Do you use illness as an excuse to avoid responsibilities or to get attention or sympathy?

47. In business relationships, write out your resentments toward bosses and co-workers.

    a. Do you feel jealous of them?

    b. Are you concerned that others in your office will get more money or prestige than you will?

    c. Do you try to prove you can "take it" on a job that is rough and tough?

    d. Do you complain about how hard you must work?

    e. List all the negative feelings you have about the people involved in your
work life.

    f. Are you indifferent and/or careless on your job?

    g. Do you think you should be the boss?

    h. Do you use the excuse that your boss, or your family or friends, shouldn't
expect so much of you?

    i. Are you able to laugh at yourself for sometimes trying to be other than that
which you are?

    j. Do you feel good about yourself when you complete a job because you want to finish it?

48. If you are divorced, or getting one, write out your negative feelings about the situation and the people involved. Resentments, fears, guilts, etc., concerning your relationship with your mate, including feelings about your children.

    a. Do you expect the children to make a decision on which parent they love the best?

    b. How well are you able to accept situations you cannot change?

    c. Are you able to back away from conflict and confusion?

49. If married, write out exactly how you feel about your spouse and children.

    a. Are they living up to your expectations?

    b. What are your expectations?

50. Do you feel that no one really understands you?

51. Is your need for affection so intense that the demands for it may be exhausting in a sexual relationship?

52. Are your expectations unreasonable?

53. How do you think you would be different if "they" were out of your life?

54. Are you uncomfortable in social situations?
    a. Do you have trouble introducing people to each other?
    b. Are you able to relax or do you find relaxing difficult?

55. Do you still feel different from other members of the program or apart from them?
    a. Do you feel superior or inferior?
    b. Do you avoid looking at yourself by making statements such as, "Oh well, some of us are sicker than others?"

56. Do you judge or make fun of people who appear to be less fortunate mentally, physically, or morally than you think you are?

57. Do you compare yourself to others to make yourself suffer by picking people who are further along in the program than you, or people who are talented in areas you are not?

58. Are you able to accept the facts of a situation, thereby deciding what to do about it?

59. The only person you can adequately compare yourself to is yourself:
    a. How were you five days ago?
    b. Five weeks ago?
    c. Five months ago?

d. At your first meeting?
e. How are you now?

60. List every act you swore you would take to the grave, disclosing to no one. Be open and honest. (Remember, life gave us all good and bad experiences. Usually the things you are most ashamed of are the very acts that made you try to grow into something of someone better. If you want freedom, you have to let go of it all.

61. In what ways are you the responsible person?

62. Are you a tightwad?
    a. What are your fears concerning money?
    b. Do you spend money with no thought of tomorrow?
    c. Are you heavily in debt?

63. Do you try to fill your life with the gratification of impulses?

64. Is your personal appearance particularly careless or prideful?
    a. On sight, do you judge people by their appearance (whether sloppy or neat)?
    b. Are you never satisfied with yourself or others?

65. What things make you feel greedy, envious, and angry?

66. Do you strive for wealth or reputation, or both, to the exclusion of other values in life?

67. Are you scornful of ideas that weren't your own?

68. Do you tell others how bad you have been or are, or do you go to the other

extreme and tell people how great you are or were? (The first communication can be pride in reserves; the second can be a way to give your ego a false sense of security).

69. Write your feelings for parents, brothers, sisters, and other family members.
	a. What resentments or hates do you still have?
	b. What still makes you feel guilty about them?

70. Do you pad your expense account or use household money to buy things for yourself?

71. Do you feel resentment toward another member of the program?

72. What kinds of things do you lie about the most?

73. Do you still need to play the Big Shot?

74. Do you strive for success in a desperate effort to deny inner needs, to repel the feelings of emptiness?

75. Are you hurt when people turn away and won't play your games?

76. Do you resent not getting as much attention as you did when you were brand new in the program?

77. Do you worry about other people's Higher Power not being as good as yours?
	a. Or maybe even better?
	b. How do you feel about people who claim to be Godly?

78. What is your conception of "God as you understand Him"?

79. Are you comparing yourself with others in spiritual growth?

    a. Have you known someone who had a spiritual approach you wish you had?

    b. Do you feel superior or inferior spiritually?

80. Do you still feel guilty about masturbation?

81. Do you feel superior because you have more education, money, brains, the "right color skin", social background, vocation, or any other seeming advantages?

    a. List your feelings of superiority.

82. Do you feel inferior because you have less of the above?

    a. List your feelings of inferiority.

83. Do you think you are superior to the general run of people?

    a. List all the ways in which you are different.

84. Do you think you are inferior to the general run of people?

    a. List all the ways in which you are different.

85. Do you have a hard time getting to places on time?

86. Do you resent others who don't seem to have problems finding happiness?

87. Are you aware of any clear adult goals?

88. Do you seek enjoyment or entertainment of one kind or another but are rarely capable of thorough enjoyment?

89. Do you turn play into work? (i.e. games, sports, hobbies that are not fun or relaxing).

90. Are you still judging the outside of others by the inside of you?

91. Have you bothered to ask the people who seem happy how they got that way?

92. How much time do you spend with the welfare and happiness of others?
    a. Have you learned how to hear other people, to see them, to know them?

93. Do you still envy people who do not appear to be compulsive?

94. Are you hostile because you don't like the hand life has dealt to you?

95. What are your present fears? List them.

96. How do you presently get other people's attention?
    a. Pouting?
    b. Sulking?
    c. Temper tantrums?
    d. Being extra good (and letting them know it)?
    e. Playing stupid?
    f. Frustrating others' activities?
    g. Bitching?
    h. Other ways?

End of Adulthood Section

SOME MORE QUESTIONS - HERE AND NOW

1. In addition to your compulsive behavior, what character defects contribute to your financial instability?

    a. Do you tend to be impulsive about spending money?

2. Did fear and inferiority about fitness for your job destroy your confidence and fill you with conflict?

    a. Did you try to cover up these feelings or inadequacy by bluffing, cheating,

lying, or evading responsibility?

    b. Or by griping that others failed to recognize your truly exceptional abilities?

3. Are your standards for yourself unduly high?

4. Did you overvalue yourself and play the "big shot"?

    a. Did you have such unprincipled ambition that you double-crossed and

undercut your associates?

5. Are you extravagant?

    a. Do you recklessly borrow money, caring little whether it is repaid or not?

6. Are you a penny-pincher, refusing to support your family properly?

    a. Did you try to cut corners financially?

    b. What about "quick" money deals?

The most common symptoms of emotional insecurity are worry, anger, self-pity and depression. These stem from causes, which sometimes seem to be within us, and at other times without. To take inventory in this respect we ought to consider carefully all personal relationships, which bring continuous and recurring troubles. It should be remembered that this kind of insecurity may arise in any area where instincts are threatened. Questioning directed to this end might run like this: Looking at both past and present, what sex situations have caused me anxiety, bitterness, frustration or depression? Appraising each situation carefully and fairly, can you see where you have been at fault? Did these perplexities beset you because of selfishness or unreasonable demands? Or, if your disturbance was seemingly caused by the behavior of others, why do you lack the ability to accept conditions you cannot change?

Do you feel that faith and dependency on a Higher Power is somewhat weak, even cowardly? Has your inability to accept much on faith been handicapped by obstinacy, sensitiveness, and unreasonable prejudice? Do you dissect spiritual beliefs and practices of spiritually minded persons as a basis of wholesale condemnation? What would your choice be if you fearlessly had to face the proposition that God either is or He isn't? These are the sorts of fundamental inquiries that can disclose the source of your discomfort and indicate whether you are able to alter you own conduct and so adjust yourself to self-discipline. Suppose a particular insecurity constantly arouses the same feelings again and again. You can ask to what extent your own mistakes have fed your gnawing anxieties, and if the actions of others are part of the cause, what can you do about that? If you are unable to change the present state of affairs, are you willing to take the measures necessary to shape your life conditions as they are?

ACCEPTANCE OF SELF

Am I really willing to forgive myself? It takes a great deal of humility to be ready for the final phase of your inventory. If we accept ourselves as we are, with all our shortcomings as revealed in our inventory, we can go to another human being with our inventory and reveal all there is to know about ourselves. If we are truly humble in the sense that we are beginning to rely increasingly on our Higher Power in more of our affairs, then we are ready for the last phase.   If you made your appointment you need only to keep that appointment and verbally discuss every portion of your inventory.

Difficulties commonly experienced are:

1. Will the other person keep my inventory in confidence?
2. Will the other person laugh at me?
3. Will the other person think me silly?
4. Will the other person think me ridiculous?
5. Will the other person think me weird?
6. Will the other person think me despicable?
7. Will the other person think me base?
8. Will the other person become disgusted with me?
9. Will the other person reject me?

In taking your inventory you wrote down all these fears realizing they stem from our need to present a "good" image of ourselves to everyone. We fear that if we don't, they will have nothing to do with us. We will be isolated and outcast and, therefore, worthless. On closer examination, it is the need to "doctor" or distort our image which has been the real barrier between us and the rest of the world, which in fact do isolate us in spite-or because-of the false front we present. Nothing draws us to others, and others to us like honesty and humility. They represent true humanity and that is what really attracts us to each other.

REWARDS INCLUDE

1. Feeling more a part of the human race.
2. Closer to our fellows.

3. Self worth increases.
4. A sense of well being comes over us as never before.
5. We get an inkling of what serenity can be.

In the past four years, I have seen some very sad stories. I know a woman in her forties that cannot and will not give herself to the program. Every time I see her she reminds me where I can be if I am not careful.

She has a large family that needs her and unfortunately the children will be one of two extremes in adulthood. I am not saying there is no hope. As, I am hopeful that not every child of addicted parents has to be like that. However, for some addiction is learned and or genetic. I have not met anyone in addiction that didn't have addiction somewhere in the family tree.

Addiction is a very challenging disease, as most that go to rehab for the wrong reasons, do not stay long. A lot of people get into recovery to try to fix things like relationships, families, and things that alcoholism and addiction have tarnished. People end up in meetings and such to get the kids back, the only problem is in order to stay one must be in recovery for himself.

Challenging as it maybe in early recovery, whether it is guilt and shame or to just get the heat off. There are a lot of ruts that I see people get into over and over again. The newcomer with thirty days trying to get financial items that have been ruined over years fixed over night. Or the newcomer that finally feels bad that their drug of choice made them do things against the law. Or the newcomer that hasn't worked the first step or found a sponsor but they are apologizing to everyone for everything they did in their past. This is dangerous territory for a newcomer in recovery.

That is why it is suggested to do ninety meetings in ninety days and to find someone to work the steps with. Some of the things that people get so caught up with little time are the concept of a higher power, making amends, anger, resentments, violence, and the deep dark places that our addiction took us. I wish you could just come into the program work all the steps in thirty days and you immediately stopped taking life and yourself so seriously, that you forgave everyone that you hurt or hurt you, and life just became perfect because you stop drinking and or doing drugs.

Honestly, those first thirty days were horrible for me. I was physically and psychologically sick. My whole body ached. Hardly anybody that I called up on the phone would take my calls. I was still lying and trying to manipulate things.

I didn't hit the meetings until I had about sixty days of continuous sobriety, as it took me that long to detox. When I went to the meetings I wasn't sure I had a problem. After the fog started rising in about two weeks of not using, I didn't want anything that was being offered to me. I refused to see that these people in the rooms were just like me. I wasn't looking for the similarities. Even though it was me that had to show up to meetings if I wanted a roof over my head. So, somehow I had gotten myself into this mess and I thought I could just pretend and eventually I could go back to where I had been. Since my old way of life was easy. I didn't have to hold a job when I was loaded. I wasn't buying this productive member of society garbage when I first came around. I had never been a productive member of society and I sure didn't want to be a square. Honestly, even after all the things I had done out there and the heat I was feeling as I had some serious consequences, I still wanted the easy way out.

In early recovery for myself, I had made some bad choices in my relapse. I had hurt people that were trying to help me. I had bill collectors calling me every day. I never thought in early recovery that there would be a day that the bill collectors weren't calling me. Today, I have a good life. I finally have stability. Of course, it comes with a price.

If only I had known that life could be this good, but I truly believe that for me, it wasn't on my time. As, nothing ever happens on my time. There was a long period of time where I thought all I deserved was to be a sick addict and that I would only be that.

There was a time I thought once an addict always an addict. I know a hand full of women that lived what I consider the roughest life out there as they lived on the street. They don't chase their drug of choice today. They have beautiful families today, and they help people when they can.

When I was " out there" I didn't care about other people. I didn't like women, cause don't you know they all were only interested in taking whatever I thought I had. I never had any friends, true friends. Back then, they only would come by if I was paying for the party, or if I had something for them that they wanted. None of those people were ever around when I truly needed them.

When I was "out there" I had no idea what a spiritual principle was. I didn't know that intimacy could occur between two men. Intimacy meaning really getting to know someone and knowing them well, like being able to look my friends today in the eyes. I never looked anyone in the eye until I was in recovery. I never held my significant others hand or supported him through a tough time. I never had any idea how good it would feel to love someone and know they loved me back. I have had so many awesome things happen thanks to the program of recovery.

There were things that when I got to recovery I thought I would never get to the other side of. I never thought I would be able to forgive my enemies. My sick mind when I got here thought I was going to have to let people step on me. I don't have to have relationships with people that are toxic to me. Today I don't talk to my father because he and I just don't jive. I forgive him today, but that doesn't give me the go ahead to allow him to hurt me any more. Today, I have decent relationships with people that are healthy and I have worthwhile and healthy relationships.

For a long time, when I first got sober, I kept asking God why stuff kept happening. I had this resentment with God about the bipolar. I couldn't understand that I had to learn lessons in life, and sometimes it's not my lesson to learn. Today, I understand that God doesn't make junk, and I am not damaged goods. So, I have some challenges and I have to work hard. Life on life's terms happens.

For me, the steps are very important, and finding a higher power seems to be the core of recovery. A lot of people get confused and think that finding a higher power is involving religion. When recovery is a spiritual thing and in no way involving organized religion. The steps are in a certain order for a reason. So, you must believe you qualify for the program before you turn your will over. When I got to the rooms, I wasn't buying the god stuff. I truly wasn't interested. At the time I thought God had left me when he was never gone. He was right there with me.

The question that is most commonly asked is, how does one get sober, what is the process? This is a powerful question. As, people are very different. What works for most people may not work for some. What worked for me may not work for the next person.

However, I can address what works for most alcoholics/addicts. For most people, rehab works. They go through what is shown in the movies 28 days starring Sandra Bullock, as that is one of my favorites. Some other videos that are helpful are My Name is Bill W, and Clean and Sober starring Michael Keaton. The reason I have listed those is that these are very good for family members, and anyone dealing with alcoholism, Alanon or any other similar item.

Recovery is a very challenging thing. It is said that it is a simple program for complicated people. However, there are many things that come up when the alcoholic/addict overcomes the cravings and are given a daily reprieve from their old way of life. As, once this occurs most people in recovery find out they have other addictions not limited to gambling, shopping addictions, relationship problems and other items that require counseling, and other forms of outside help.

AA was the first twelve-step program and was the source and has been the model for all similar recovery groups such as Gamblers Anonymous, Emotions Anonymous, Narcotics Anonymous, Sexaholics Anonymous, Sex Addicts Anonymous, Overeaters Anonymous, and Al-Anon/Alateen, among others. I just wanted to let people understand that in my opinion everyone in society is recovering from something. Whether it is violence, abuse, alcoholism, addiction, emotional problems or physical challenges. In our fast paced lives, to be human means you are dealing with something.

One of the things I have held onto in the program is that I do this program of recovery no matter what. As, there is no good reason for me to pick up. No matter if I am going through something painful, no matter if I loose the relationship, get the relationship, loose the job, loose a ton of money, no matter what happens that I feel isn't fair, I have no reason to get loaded today.

The cut and dry is that I am an addicted person and I "enjoy" doing stupid things, as crazy as that sounds. Today, I just don't like the actions, decisions, and the consequences that I pay that involve this.

Another thing that hit me hard in early recovery is that I never have to drink or drug again if I don't want to. Meaning that in my mind, living my new way of life or my old way of life is a choice today. I have way too many blessings today, to loose over a quick fix. As, I would simply loose everything, over one moment of being drunk and/or high. The consequences are just too large today for me.

I don't exactly know what God's will for me is today, as far as the big picture. Though, I know what Gods will for me is not. I know living a decent life has a lot to do with it. I know living on the street is not God's will. Today gods will for me is to have good things happen and to live a life that I could never imagine is Gods' will.

A tool that I have today is writing. I consider writing therapy for myself today. I can be in the worst funk, write about it, process it, talk about it with my sponsor, and work through today's challenges. I'm finding out that the little things that bother me are just little things that get under my skin.

The way I look at recovery today is if someone as sick as I was can find recovery, there must be something to this deal. As long as I do what the literature suggests and I practice the steps daily, and I keep trying, generally life for me is good. I also look at all the people that I get to work with in the rooms as an opportunity. As, for so long, I didn't have friends. People didn't care about what I was doing in the world of addiction. I also didn't care about anyone but myself when I was in my addiction. Which shows that recovery is about change.

Another important point is the difference between medication and drugs. Medication is what I take to get better when I am sick and I take as prescribed. Drugs are what I take when life sucks and I am stuffing my feelings and I am hurting others and myself. I have seen many people die that do not understand this. As a addicts mind and body do not know the difference between being sick and taking medication and just taking drugs to get away from it all and running from themselves.

I find the idea of ninety meetings in ninety days a very good concept. The reason I harp on this is I learned a lot in going to a lot of meetings at first, and I was able to find someone to work the steps with. I understand that asking someone to sponsor a newcomer is challenging. The deal is you don't have to be friends, some do become close friends, but all don't. This is just someone that walks you through the process. Also, it's not a thing that is set in stone. I have been sober for four years, and I have gone through more sponsors than carter has pills. I honestly had a hard time working with the woman, as I had never liked dealing with women. However with time and by working the twelve steps, traditions, etc I have walked through the whole friends with women challenge.

I had to work a lot of fourth steps to be ok with looking myself in the mirror and not seeing a complete mess. My current sponsor has been all right with this. For me, the fourth and fifth steps have saved my life. It has allowed me to not just work the first couple of steps and quit.

We are often informed that we have come into the world of the spirit by taking steps 1-9. We developed fresh sane relationships with ourselves with a higher power and with others. We now have conscious contact with such higher power. We know how to act when our defects surface and we make mistakes, since we have practiced steps 1-9. Which is much talked about our tools in our toolbox. We have started a new life. We will continue to practice these spiritual principles, the steps, and incorporate them in our life as long as we live.

Anyone that says that the fourth and fifth steps cause relapse are lying to himself or herself. The steps allow for freedom. What typically happens to those in this situation is they continue to have things that they are prepared to take with them to the grave, or they are not being honest with themselves. I will admit that the first twelve steps one works with a sponsor are very hard. A lot of people think they just throw up everything the first time through the twelve steps. Which is totally not a requirement. I personally believe that if you work a thorough first step and you don't have reservations anything is possible. The rest of the steps can be worked and gone back to at a later date. As I can be alright with a step one week and another week, something may come up and I may need to do more pencil and paper, which is totally fine. As, life on life's terms happens.

A Few excerpts of the fourth step

This information came from friends and sponsees.

I had no understanding of how much resentment I actually had. Doing my Fourth Step was a factual eye opener. As until I was in recovery, I never saw the true truth in anything, as I only heard and saw what I wanted to. I was blaming multiples of people for lots of things and never resolving any issues. I wasn't even looking for a solution or believing that today in recover I could live in the solution. As, keep allowing things to just keep building up inside of me. There is a saying that people say, "resentments are like taking poison and expecting the other person to die." That's exactly how I felt, poisoned by my individual resentments. I was living in a prison that I had made by myself.

It took all of the faith and trust I built in the Program by working the first three Steps, to get sufficient courage to be honest and truly explore the truth about myself in the Fourth Step. It was very important to be able to face and walk through my fear and to be able to reach out and ask my sponsor for advice and support. To be able to swallow my pride, self-centeredness, and to see my disease for what it is and to be able t o use the tools my sponsor has given me in the first three steps and to move on instead of staying stuck. I suggest to anyone that they do the Steps in sequence, as they are numbered for a reason.

The Fourth Step isn't about a list of every bad thing we ever did, even though it may start out that way. Mine did, but then I started looking for patterns and so I rewrote my Fourth step and grouped items that were of a similar pattern. Under these groupings I tried to condense the particular pattern or defect of character I found down into a simple line or two. As, it's those patterns, improper coping mechanisms, and faulty beliefs that are necessary to discuss with a sponsor in the Fifth Step.

A few excepts of the fifth steps

My Fifth Step was a complete conscious life changing, life-affirming breakthrough. It was the first time in my life that I had ever been capable of honestly sharing who I really was on a genuine level with another human being. It was the beginning of the end of a life of feeling somehow different than, and isolated from, everyone else. It was the point where I finally felt a sense of truly fitting in with the human race. It was the first time I felt true acceptance and honest kindness for myself. When I think of my experience with my first Fifth Step I recall the results more than the process. It seemed less like something I did than something that simply happened to me.

The strangest thing happened to me when I shared my Fifth Step with my sponsor. I read off my list of resentments, my assets, my values and where I felt that I'd fallen short, my secrets, all those items and it felt really good to get rid of all that garbage. Though, when I was almost done I saw how much resentment I had for my bi-polar illness, immediately seeing all of my loss and pain. I was in tears in no time, just trying to explain how much that hurt and how unfair it was. None of that had been included in my Fourth Step but it was the thing that had been consuming me the most and I hadn't included it in my step work. This became an item to work on thanks to the steps I can find peace of mind in my recovery today, and this doesn't have to be something I hold onto or use behind.

Picking just the right person to share your Fifth Step with is really important. As, Spouses, lovers, and family members should not be considered because these people are often too close and might be hurt or unable to see things from that close perspective that someone with a bit more objectivity and distance might see. Sponsors are good as long as they have experience and really understand the Steps. Many therapists and clergy have training and experience with the Steps and can be wonderful resources. The important thing about using sponsorship with this step is that the trust necessary exists.

As a sponsor, it's not my purpose to form opinions in which a person who shares their Fourth Step work with me. I simply listen quietly, sometimes asking for clarification, and occasionally I share my experiences. The point is not to focus on myself, but to offer another perspective or insight. Taking another members Fifth Step is a huge honor. To me it's an almost sacred honor. I remember how scared I was when I shared my first Fifth Step. I felt awkward and was worried that my sponsor might think less of me because of my past behavior. Some of that stuff was so embarrassing. Yet she listened to every word and in the end gave me a hug and told me how proud she was of me. She actually said it was an honor and thanked me for trusting her. That's the gift I want to pass along.

Spirituality is the way we acquaint ourselves with a higher power. It is the way we allow for meaning in our lives. It is the recognition of the presence of Spirit within us and a development of a style of life consistent with that presence. Spirituality allows for a perspective to promote purpose, meaning, and direction in life. It may find words and similarities through religion but is not religion.

Getting motivated, is often referred to as getting into action. Generally, most addicts suffer from a variety of mental and emotional issues as well as physical addictions. They have a lack of self-esteem, inferiority complexes and overblown egos on top of these. It is said that you can take the alcohol away from the alcoholic but underneath that is a lot of hurt, anger, resentment and years of built up defense. We will never grow in our recovery or grow into the people we want to become without seeking self-improvement. This means taking the initiative and getting into rigorous action of working on one's self-improvement on a daily basis.

Religion is a system of beliefs, values, rules for conduct and rituals. It is a way a person's spirituality is expressed. Ideally, religion provides an atmosphere for spiritual development.

Affirmations

. . .

Some Examples of Meditations

SHAME

"It is not the criminal things that are hardest to confess,
But the ridiculous and the shameful."
Jean Jacques Rousseau

I had a very strange childhood filled with lots of emotional and physical neglect. Combine that with moving about once a year and being deemed as "unacceptable" by each new community we moved into, and how could I help but feel a great sense of shame about everything about me?

As an adult I left home and became a well-respected part of a new community. I have lived in the same nice house, with a beautiful yard, and had well kept-children. In spite of all the evidence to the contrary, internally I was still that "unacceptable" child. I had not told anyone about my childhood because I felt it to be a shameful secret. I thought that much of my adult unhappiness was deserved because I truly believed that even though no one knew the truth about me, deep down I really was still unacceptable.

Since beginning recovery, I have been releasing something far more important than the 60 pounds of weight I have lost. I have begun to release the shame, the sense of being unacceptable, and the sense of being unworthy and unlovable. I have shared my secrets with wonderfully loving, accepting people. By sharing my secrets I am releasing my pain. My request that my name not be revealed at the end of this meditation, though, clearly states that I still have work to do. TRG, the program, and the steps are offering me the means to recovery and I will gratefully accept the offer!

One day at a time...
I will remember that the old false self-perceptions are no longer relevant in my life. I am learning new ways of self-acceptance and new ways of self-nurturing that will serve me far better.
~ Karen A.

COMPULSIONS
"All human actions have one or more of these seven causes: chance, nature, compulsion, habit, reason, passion, desire."
Aristotle
When I was eating compulsively, it was similar to taking nitrous oxide at my dentist. Like a heavy anesthesia, the food comforted me and gave me an extraordinary sense of well-being. Like many short-term cures for what is bothering us, it took its toll. Any resemblance to reality while in the fog of compulsive eating is purely coincidental. While there may be times in my life I needed anesthesia, to use it day in and day out to block emotional pain is a burden only compulsive eaters know about.

Compulsion is self-will gone berserk. I try to think of it as the opposite of effortless abstinence. Between the two are miles and miles of varying experiences. For me there was never moderation ... only the two extremes. It took several years of squeaky-clean abstinence to trust myself and begin to try moderation in eating. At that point I had learned to recognize and be aware of the dangers of that first compulsive bite. There has been times when this cunning disease is always waiting to pounce and has sent me straight back to hell as a result of that one single compulsive bite.

One day at a time...
I will pray that my actions are caused by anything except compulsions.
~ Mari
One Day HABITS
"A habit cannot be tossed out the window;
It must be coaxed down the stairs a step at a time."
Mark Twain

How grateful I was when I read that quote – even though I had to translate it a bit. It has always been difficult for me to start good habits. I've heard all kinds of things about that – that it takes 21 days, 40 days, or an x-number of weeks to start a habit. It always made me feel bad and different because I swear for me, it probably takes at least two years. Until then I'd be biting my nails, knowing that even if I did practice good habits, they might disappear at any time. It was supposed to be so much faster, so much easier! A few weeks of eating healthy, and magically I would be cured! Well, that never happened.

Now I can look at good habits – like eating healthy, exercising, meditating, paying my bills on time – as tender, shy little animals that need a long time before they can be coaxed up the stairs of my life. They need patience, a lot of quiet time, and a willingness to be understood and studied. How do I feed, nurture and care for this habit?

I cannot do it alone. I do not have the patience, the willingness, nor the nurturing to do this by myself. I need the help of the fellowship and the help of my Higher Power. This help is freely given to me ~ all I need to do is accept it, and together we can make my habits more and more comfortable in the house of my life.

One day at a time...
With the help of my Higher Power and the program, I can patiently learn to practice healthy habits.
~ Isabella

FAITH

"Faith is not belief. Belief is passive.
Faith is active."
Edith Hamilton
I always believed that God could relieve my suffering if He chose; however, I was overlooking the distinction of the required "partnership" between my choices and his strength. God is not a magician who, with artful finesse, will relieve me of the bondage of my free-will choices. He requires my attention -- and then my ACTION -- in order to work through and in my life.

One day at a time...
I am willing to test my faith by putting forth the required action(s) that will help me move toward my share of miracles that abound in this Program.
~ January K.
Learning New Ideas
"I can't understand why people are frightened of new ideas.
I'm frightened of the old ones."- John Cage

When I look back upon my life before I heard of food being a compulsion, I remember my old thinking -- which was not very thoughtful at all! I performed the task of feeding myself without any conscious forethought or planning. It was whatever was in sight, available, or easiest to fix. I never stopped to think why I eat what I eat. I don't know what I was thinking when I consumed something that I knew would leave me feeling as though I were in a stupor or would send me crashing into naps that lasted hours.

My old ideas were mindless, thoughtless. I was an unhealthy automaton who had never been taught how to think about the "what" and "why" of her food choices. I have learned to listen to others who have recovery, take what I need from their stories, and apply some of their actions to my own life.

One day at a time...

I am willing to put aside old ideas as I discover them, to lay groundwork for the new ideas that have been presented to me, and to continue on a journey of personal growth. My mind is like a garden. I have to pull the weeds so that new flowers can begin to grow.

~ January K.

Today I will be free of alcohol and other intoxicating drugs

Today I will follow a plan to manage my emotional or psychiatric illness

Today I will practice the twelve steps

Anonymous

Footsteps
She walked along a different path
Searching for an explored trail
She found some new paths
But she refused to take them
Though they seemed inviting
She preferred to follow footsteps

Not repeating her mistakes
She didn't take a chance this time
History didn't repeat itself...-Anonymous

Footprints in the Sand

One night I dreamed I was walking along the beach with the Lord. Many scenes from my life flashed across the sky.

In each scene I noticed footprints in the sand. Sometimes there were two sets of footprints, other times there was one only.

This bothered me because I noticed that during the low periods of my life, when I was suffering from anguish, sorrow or defeat, I could see only one set of footprints, so I said to the Lord,

"You promised me Lord,
That if I followed you, you would walk with me always. But I have noticed that during the most trying periods of my life there has only been one set of footprints in the sand. Why, when I needed you most, have you not been there for me?"

The Lord replied, "The years when you have seen only one set of footprints, my child, is when I carried you."-Anonymous

Butt Prints In The Sand
One night I had a wondrous dream,
One set of footprints there was seen,
The footprints of my precious Lord,
But mine were not along the shore.
But then some stranger prints appeared,
And I asked the Lord, "What have we here?"

Those prints are large and round and neat,
"But Lord they are too big for feet."

"My child," He said in somber tones,
"For miles I carried you alone.
I challenged you to walk in faith,
But you refused and made me wait."

"You disobeyed, you would not grow,
The walk of faith, you would not know.
So I got tired, I got fed up,
And there I dropped you on your butt."

"Because in life, there comes a time,
When one must fight, and one must climb.
When one must rise and take a stand,
Or leave their butt prints in the sand."- Anonymous

The Full Version of the Serenity Prayer
God, grant me the Serenity
To accept the things I cannot change...
Courage to change the things I can,
And Wisdom to know the difference.
Living one day at a time,
Enjoying one moment at a time,
Accepting hardship as the pathway to peace.
Taking, as He did, this sinful world as it is,
Not as I would have it.
Trusting that He will make all things right
if I surrender to His will.
That I may be reasonably happy in this life,
And supremely happy with Him forever in the next.
Amen.
Attributed to Reinhold Neibuhr

Dear God,
I pray again
As I so often do
That I might have the
Serenity
To accept the things
I simply cannot
And should not
Change. –Anonymous

Dear God,
Please help me to accept people, places and things.
Help me to know the meaning of true acceptance,
Most of all help me to accept the things I cannot change-
Anonymous
Dear God,
I am so far from
Perfect. I pray this
Prayer so often. Help
Me to focus on those
Special words in it.
Serenity.
Accept.
Courage.
Wisdom.
Grant me the
SERENITY
To accept the things
I cannot change ~
COURAGE
To change the
Things I can;
And
WISDOM
to know the difference.

Living ONE DAY AT A TIME;
Enjoying one moment at a time;
Accepting hardship as the
Pathway to peace.
Taking this
Sinful world as it IS,
Not as I would have it.
Trusting that He will make
All things right if I
Surrender to His Will;
That I may be reasonably happy
In this life, and supremely
Happy forever in
The next. -Anonymous
Third Step Prayer

God, I offer myself to Thee — to build with me and to do with me as Thou wilt. Relieve me of the bondage of self, that I may better do Thy will. Take away my difficulties, that victory over them may bear witness to those I would help of Thy Power, Thy Love, and Thy Way of life. May I do Thy will always -Anonymous

Seventh Step Prayer

My Creator, I am now willing that you should have all of good, bad & me. I pray that you now remove from me every single defect of character, which stands in the way of my usefulness to you & my fellows. Grant me strength, as I go out from here to do your bidding.-Anonymous

Eleventh Step Prayer

Lord, make me a channel of thy peace--that where there is hatred, I may bring love--that where there is wrong, I may bring the spirit of forgiveness--that where there is discord, I may bring harmony--that where there is error, I may bring truth--that where there is doubt, I may bring faith--that where there is despair, I may bring hope--that where there are shadows, I may bring light--that where there is sadness, I may bring joy. Lord, grant that I may seek rather to comfort than to be comforted--to understand, than to be understood--to love, than to be loved. For it is by self-forgetting that one finds. It is by forgiving that one is forgiven. It is by dying that one awakens to eternal life.

Serenity Prayer

GOD, grant me the serenity to accept the things I cannot change, Courage to change the things I can, and the wisdom to know the difference. Living ONE DAY AT A TIME; Enjoying one moment at a time; Accepting hardship as the pathway to peace. Taking, as He did, this sinful world as it is, not as I would have it. Trusting that He will make all things right if I surrender to His Will; That I may be reasonably happy in this life, and supremely happy with Him forever in the next.

St Francis Prayer

Lord, make me a channel of thy peace, that where there is hatred, I may bring love; that where there is wrong, I may bring the spirit of forgiveness; that where there is discord, I may bring harmony; that where there is error, I may bring truth; that where there is doubt, I may bring faith; that where there is despair, I may bring hope; that where there are shadows, I may bring light that where there is sadness, I may bring joy.

Lord, grant that I may seek rather to comfort than to be comforted; to understand, than to be understood; to love, than to be loved. For it is by self-forgetting that one finds. It is by forgiving that one is forgiven.

It is by dying that one awakens to Eternal Life. - Anonymous